Help! I'm Coaching

and Discipline Do I Need To Know?

Written By Cory Moore

Contents

1. Prologue

2. Getting Started

3. More Basics

4. Drills Scrimmages and Applications

5. Gameplay and Rules

6. Goalies, Sweepers, Strikers

7. Making it Competitive

8. Discipline and Parent Engagement

9. Rules

10. Games Drills and Useful

Prologue

I started coaching soccer as a way to be involved in the community 12 years ago. It was before I had kids of my own. I had no idea what I was doing or how to get the kids to act civil much less how to get them to learn. I asked a college buddy to be my assistant. He helped, but he knew less than I did. Each year since I've been able to take what I learned and build some pretty good teams. I now coach my own sons' teams. Sometimes the fact that I have one of my own on the team is an advantage, sometimes a hindrance. The little monsters drive me out of my mind at the beginning of the season. Hopefully you won't have a single lazy, coddled, or stubborn little monster but if you do - I'll show you how to turn the tides from the start to teach them sportsmanship, game etiquette, and the basics of soccer. Stick with me and we'll go over strategies to take a mediocre team to one that can compete. As in all things you will need to know the basics before you can move into the strategies and formations, but I promise you will learn what you need in this concise guide to leading a team of young ones on a soccer field.

I have been on a soccer field in one capacity or another for over thirty years. The game itself hasn't changed much but the way we learn to play it has. Remember the old drill we used to see or use where we put 10 cones in a straight line and dribbled around them and back weaving in between? Yeah. We don't do that anymore. Don't laugh. If you haven't been around the "experts" in the last few years you can't see why that drill isn't a no brainer. It still helps with all sorts of skills but now we know how to get the skills and habits of that drill at 1000% more effective rate.

One thing we see year after year is the number of kids playing soccer dwindles as they reach 13-14 years old. We believe this happens for a few reasons that can't be helped and a few that could. If more coaches took the time to learn just a little bit more then we could give these kids a better experience and keep them interested in soccer longer. Kudos to you for learning the difference between being a free babysitter and an effective coach. Let's get started.

Getting Started

There are only a few things you need to coach soccer - a place to play, a couple of soccer balls, and some players. Sounds simplistic, right? Well it really is all you need. You might want the latest gadgets and training DVDs but your players will learn more from watching and repeating than you can imagine. There are all sorts of resources out there for specific drills and formations on the internet for each age group. You do not- I repeat DO NOT need to know all of that to get your team started. If you push yourself into learning all of the technical jargon too soon you will not enjoy your time with the kids. Please do not pressure yourself with all of that if you are just getting started. I started with knowledge of the rules and that's about it. My best team ever didn't know a single technical term. We'll go through the stuff you need in the first few chapters.

If you know how to lead your team through a few good practices you will be able find out who has experience and who is more clueless than you. Once you know who has some experience you can ask them to show the others the simple stuff that everyone will need such as a "throw in". I'll go over that important step a little later - even 4 year olds need to know this one. Giving the players a foundation of basics will help them later and give you something to build on. You will see the group grow in skill and knowledge with every practice so don't worry if you have a group of 7 year olds that just know they are supposed to score in "that" goal. That's a start.

In this chapter we will go through hosting your first practice in two easy steps. By the end of chapter one you will be able to have a starting point for your season. Most areas have a fall season and spring season with the team kept together for both. That gives you almost 6 months of time with these players. You'll want to make sure the players are having fun while learning. That's step one. Have fun while learning.

Have fun while learning - kids love to play anything. Most all of the drills or teaching moments come while "playing" something in soccer. You can even make the introductions fun. I like to gather everyone up and have them take a knee. I have had to teach them how to do that sometimes. This little step will give you a way to get their attention. If they come together on one knee they know it's time to listen. They feel like part of a team and that will help them later. Then I like to have them YELL their name to everyone. Do it a few times because you need to be able to say good job Ben or Sarah Beth. Everybody likes to yell and they need to know that on the field they don't have to be quiet. Once you've done your introductions you are ready for some soccer. Usually just pairing them up to pass the ball back and forth will help you separate out who has experience. As soon as you can tell put the ones who are close to the same level of control and strength together. There's nothing more frustrating than having to pass back and forth with someone who can't get the ball back to you if you put it right at their feet. Older siblings, maturity level, and natural talent all factor in to the level of the players to start a season. The smallest kid on one my teams had more skill than I'd ever seen from a 7 year old. Come to find out he was 5 and playing up an age division. He ended up not being fast enough to really have an advantage but man could he control the ball.

Teach the basics- I mean the basics. Depending on your age level you may need to teach them to not use their hands. That's ok. Some have never played or even seen a soccer ball. Start with how to dribble the ball. This is easy sounding, but it is almost never corrected because fast kids can get you an advantage. The problem is the players start out thinking they just kick the ball and go get it. That is <u>WRONG</u>. Even for the youngest groups you need to teach them to keep the ball close to them. It takes a lot of practice and time to learn this especially if they are fast. The problem is there is always someone faster. When a player has to control the ball they won't be as fast as the kid catching up with them. The players need control of the ball. If they kick and chase then another player will be faster or simply closer to the ball and they will lose possession. Keeping the ball is easier than stealing so teach them control. There's not really a magic formula for this but there is a simple and fun drill for it. Remember rule one? Have fun while learning - Keep it in mind. Some will be so bad it will be funny. It's ok. Laugh. They won't know what's going on. Have the players line up in a spread out line on the midfield line all facing the same way. Have them to dribble toward the same goal but to listen for you to say "red light" or "stop" depending on their age. When they hear it they should be the first to stop and put their foot on top of the ball. It teaches them to keep the ball close. You can vary it and have them put their knee or bottom on the ball in order to keep interest. The main point is to keep it close. If one is running faster and kicking it further from himself he will be last to settle the ball and won't win this game. Push them so they aren't walking but aren't just sprinting either. This drill needs a lot of practice because no one under 13 is good enough at it. Keep it light hearted and fun and the players will get more out of that simple drill than out of an hour of scrimmage. Scrimmage has its place but only after they have learned some stuff to work on during the scrimmage.

In your first and every practice to start a season please practice throw-ins. They are easy but messed up all the time. Have the kid's pair up and throw in to each other. It helps in two ways. It helps them learn the throw in and how to stop a moving ball (settle the ball) so the receiving player can get control of it. The only rules for a legal throw in are to use both hands at the same, keep both feet on the ground at all times, and bring the ball straight back behind your head and straight back over your head. Keeping it straight means it will not spin to the side when released. It has to go all the way close to your neck when you bring it back. You can drag a foot while throwing it in but start with flat footed throw INS until they know you can't jump while throwing in. They must pay attention to foot placement. Then when they get that they can move to dragging a foot to give them more forward momentum. It's more important to not give possession to the other team for a bad throw in than to throw it a mile.

The other half of that drill comes into play with the receiving player. Have them throw in low and the other player will start to realize how to give a little cushion with their foot to stop the ball. You don't want it bouncing off of you every time because you have to chase it down. Do this for a few minutes and they will naturally start figuring it out. Nobody likes chasing the balls they don't have to. Explain to use a little cushion and they will get. Have them throw it a little higher to each other and practice the cushion with their thighs, chest, and even their foreheads. All of the first few practices should incorporate these drills to get these skills down pat. The skills come with practice and I bet you don't have any who have been doing this stuff on their own at home. How many parents know to teach this stuff? Very few. If they did we would have more eager soccer coaches. You know the basics now! These drills should be followed up with a scrimmage and remind them to use this stuff in the scrimmage. If possible break the scrimmage down to the smallest number of players on each team so each player gets more touches on the ball than if 22 players are sharing one ball. If you scrimmage most of practice you haven't given them enough repetition to learn the basics. The current thought is it takes 2,000 repetitions to master a move so your body can do it while you're thinking of something else (like who's open?). Those 2,000 touches need to be done right too. Keep that in mind and vary the game while having them repeat the moves.

More Basics

If you felt that last chapter was too easy you were right….. and wrong. There is a lot of stuff still to do with your team but knowing the basics and being able to perform them every time are two very different things. You've learned the fundamental basics and need to keep them in your future practices but that's only a starting part. In this chapter you will learn how to bring in more games to your practice and teach a few more fundamental skills all players will need. We won't be breaking out the cones or the mini goals just yet but by starting these drills you will see exponential growth within a short time. Keeping the players feeling like each drill is a competition will keep their interest and keep most from having a wandering mind. Who can do it best? Who can do it fastest? Who can get it right the most times? Asking these questions makes them want to do their best. It will keep order to your unruly monsters and keep you busy saying yes you are doing great. Call out each player for doing something right. Call out a winner for each drill. Try to make everyone a winner of something instead the same kid that's a little ahead. You are here to help, teach, and inspire. If they feel they don't ever get right they will stop trying. I don't believe everyone always deserves a trophy or any of that participating is winning junk but as a coach you must encourage your players to do their best. Discipline has its place but so does the encouragement.

No toe pokes! This is important. Your shoe isn't flat in the front. It's pointed. If you use your toes to kick the ball it will not have any sort of accuracy. Four year olds can learn to use the inside of their foot to pass or shoot the ball. They will get excited and forget but they forget which is right and left too so don't worry about it. The important thing is teach them how to pass back and forth using the inside of their foot. They will figure out how to do it with power and accuracy on their own. I learned a bunch of crap about how to plant my stationary foot and everything else almost to the point of how to hold my mouth while kicking growing up. The technical stuff can fine tune a player but if you trying to teach a kid to play soccer don't overload with stuff they can't do yet. Repetition will help more than anything in the world. Many Park and Rec players won't have any time with a ball without you. Teach them to use the inside of their foot and then ask them do it in the drills you run. It doesn't take long for it to become a habit and then for them to get good at it. The earlier they learn the basics the faster they can mature it. The will have to learn it later to be competitive so if they have had time to practice it when they are just learning it they will be that much further ahead.

Passing the Ball - To work on passing they must - take a guess - pass the ball. Same goes for shooting. Up until now you have your whole team doing the same thing at the same time. That keeps the boredom from creeping in. Waiting in a line bores me and I'm almost forty. I'll pull out my phone and check my email 10 times in 5 minutes waiting in line. What do you think a 6 year old will do? Watch patiently trying to learn? No sir. That's when most discipline problems start. Keeping them all involved is extremely important. It works on their fitness so you don't have to do sprints and keeps you from having to worry about the horseplay that will start within a group of kids. Almost every drill I lead involves the whole team at once. Keep that going with passing drills. It may seem simplistic but how long do you think it would take pass perfectly 2,000 times? More time than you have with the team, I can promise that. Pairing them up for passing can get old but doing it every practice is important. An easy way to vary it can be to ask them to use their left foot for a while. What? Their left foot? That just seems cruel. While the few lefties you have will enjoy it the rest will whine. They need to do it just as much with their non-dominate foot as the one they prefer. Another way to get a bunch of touches and keep them involved is to separate them into two lines. Have the lines about six feet part on the midfield line or the 18. I'll explain in a minute what the 18 is. Have the lines facing each other and the player in front of one line passes to the one in front of the other. The passing player goes to the end of the other line so he is facing the line he just left and the game continues. I know I just said I hated lines but this goes so fast they won't have time for boredom.

It looks like this.

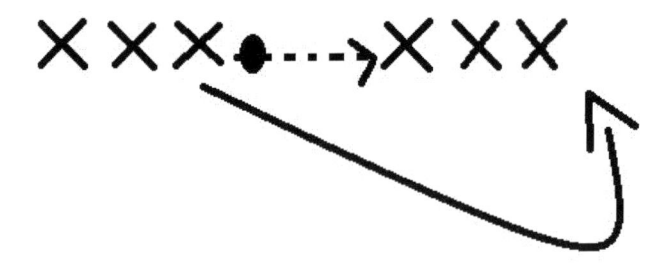

✗ ✗ ✗ •---➔ ✗ ✗ ✗

After they pass they go to the back of the other line.

Notice we haven't had them line up and shoot at the goal yet? It's slow and will cause problems. Have them all shoot at the same. That's what they will they do while they wait on practice to start all on their own. It doesn't hurt to have a little disorder. Don't slow them down with a line. Of course don't put a goalie in there to block 11 shots at once. We want them to try to find out how to put power behind a shot. They can't do that if they only get five or six times through a line. Have them stay a little farther than what distance feels just too far for them and just keep shooting. You should be behind the goal feeding the balls back to them. With a little help returning the balls you can keep them shooting and getting the practice they need to start progressing at a fast pace.

Spread them out in pairs across the field. Have them pass the ball out in front of their partner. The pairs will work their way down the field and finish with a shot on the goal. Keep them all moving so everybody is getting in some running and learning how to pass on the move. This drill is simple but if you are encouraging them and keep telling them to pass in front of their partner it will teach them passing to a moving target and how to pass while on the move themselves.

Drills, Scrimmages, and Applications

You have learned more in the last few pages than many veteran coaches know. Keeping the lines to a minimum, more touches equals better players, and teach before the scrimmage are all Mantras a soccer coach should follow. In this chapter we will see why and how to apply these procedures to the gameplay. By giving the players freedom to learn through their experiences you will see them grow so much faster than they will with strict methodology when learning basics. The drills you used to teach a throw in for example will pay off tenfold while in the game and hopefully the guys/gals had fun. While running your scrimmage be sure to stop and have a repeat if they don't use the correct form to a throw in. There is nothing more frustrating than getting called in a game for bad form on a throw in. It's simple and shouldn't get called on a coach who knows better. Practice it until they get it down and then keep doing it because the flip side (settling the throw in) is a common mistake. Most young monsters want to let the ball go by and chase it. This gives the other team a chance to get control. It's thrown to your player. He should settle it and either dribble or pass as the situation dictates. Chasing a ball when you should have possession is the lazy and wrong way of playing.

You should keep going over that until it is something they repeat to make fun of the coach. Really if they hear it enough they will do it. And they will thank you later for it.

The ball is in play, now what? There are literally thousands of games you can play to teach the players to confront the ball or steal the ball. As they get older you can teach them to place themselves between the ball and the goal. To start you have to get them used to trying to take the ball from the other team. I have my team split into two groups about 15 feet apart. I toss a ball between the first two in line and have them fight for the ball and take it to the other end of the field to score. This helps in two ways. It helps by having them run without realizing they are doing it. Sprints are punishment to a little monster but they will do this all day and ask to do it again. It also helps by giving them an entire field to challenge for the ball. Usually a challenge takes place within just a few feet on the field. Once missed the player with the ball will be slowed down enough for the rest of the defending team to gang up and take the ball away. In this drill they keep challenging until the one with the ball at the end of the field shoots at the goal. One on one is tricky because it doesn't help if you put a strong player against a weak one. The weak one won't get a thing but the run out of it. Try to pair them up with like skill level. I vary it up by putting cones down that the players have to stay inside. This forces a challenge in a tighter place and more control is needed. It's a step up and makes the hesitant ones actually challenge the ball since the other one has to dribble so close to them. You can vary this up more and play a game called sharks and minnows. It's a game I grew up playing in the swimming pools. One or two people are in the middle and the others try to cross their "zone" without being tagged but in this case we'll focus on not losing the ball. Swimming pools all across the country see this game every summer. Most kids will understand it instantly. They learn to dribble while looking for the shark. It teaches the shark to attack for the ball. If a shark kicks a ball out of the zone that minnow becomes a shark for round two until there is only one minnow and they are the winner. You play this with the whole team and no one sits out. This is a must game. Do this one often. The players will ask for it next practices. It is a gold level drill. The more practice in this are you can provide the better they will get. I am going to say it again. Do this gold level drill often! If the players can't dribble around another player they can't win. If they can't steal it from the other team - they can't win. This drill works both dribbling and stealing while running them hard at the same time.

More dribble practice! There are only a few parts to soccer. Dribble, pass, repeat, shoot for offense and defend the open field player or as the goalie defend the shot are the only parts. You can learn different ways or moves to do each thing but mainly you are doing the same thing over and over all game. If you can't dribble the ball you can't get close to the goal. You need more practice here than anywhere. Have the players start dribbling the ball inside the midfield circle without running into each other or their ball. Doing this makes them look up and not at their feet while dribbling. Do it for a minute and you'll be surprised how many touches each player in a minute. Make a game of it by placing cones in odd angled pairs in the circle. Have half of them go at a time for 45 seconds and see how many sets of cones they can navigate through without knocking one over or bumping into another players ball. They get a point for each set of cones they go through. If they bump into a ball or knock over a cone, they lose a point. Have the other half of the players count points for and against for the players doing the drill. Then switch them up. Do it three turns for each group and you've helped them get close to 1000 touches in less than five minutes. The old cone weave down and back drill could take ten minutes to get through and only provide 50 or 60 touches for each player. Each player waited in line for eight of those ten minutes. See the improvement? Half the time and 20 times the touches. By making sure we keep the players moving and touching the ball we can help them figure out how to handle different situations without outright teaching each situation. We'll go over positioning and other important stuff in the chapter on gameplay but for now each player learning how to handle the ball is the key. Without being able to handle the ball they can be in the right spots and it wouldn't accomplish a thing.

I had a player that had speed and the drive to win but couldn't figure out how to kick the ball more than ten feet. He was always in the way because he knew how to play the situation but couldn't do anything with it once he got the ball. It was frustrating to me and him. We worked on his touches with the rest of the team (no one on one coaching) and he became a MVP by the end of the spring season. When he finally scored in a game you would have thought we had won the World Cup! The parents saw how hard he worked and cheered for him as hard as they did their own children. Seeing them grow and learn is what it is all about. If small victories like that do not inspire you then you may not need to coach. We didn't win that game but they cheered, hard. We ended that season losing to a team in the district tournament with our heads held high. We fought hard to get into that tournament. We had been in last place after our highest skilled player broke his arm and came back in the standings to win a berth in the tournament. He didn't come to play in the tournament and we were playing teams that belonged in a different league but my guys never gave up. They kept playing because it was fun. They wanted to do their best for themselves, for each other, and for me. As the coach it's your job to keep telling them they can do it. I have no doubt a few of these 9 year olds will be playing high school and college soccer in the future. I've already seen some of my players go to play for the Olympic Development Program and some play at the college level. I know they worked hard well after I was part of their life. If I had been lazy or not made it fun they may have decided not to continue playing. I've taken three teams to the State Tournament and none of the college players were on those teams. Skill at 9 doesn't set their tempo for life but a foundation of enjoyment and learning the basics might. Keep your head high and be the example they need. You never know what your leadership may develop.

Gameplay and Rules

The night before your first game you may be wondering if you will know enough to just get through it. You will. Depending on the age you are coaching you may see referees or not. In the youngest age divisions the coaches usually handle the game play. It's helpful because if you are out there on the field you can direct positioning. I recommend teaching the players to play their area or position even from the youngest ages. If your star wears himself out playing the whole field he won't be any use by the end of the game. The field is just too big. Spread them out with two or three defenders and the rest acting as midfielders or as forwards to score. You need at least one good defender. You'll be tempted to use your fastest as forwards but if the ball stays close to the goal you are defending all game then what does that accomplish? I'm betting you are coaching a team with many levels of skilled players. Some will barely ever touch the ball in the game. That's ok. They will get better if you keep working with them. Build confidence and it will come. Don't use them as your only defense though. Move the players around to try them in different positions. You may find a player that will not go up to score even though they are the best ball handler. Use what they do and build on it. I watched my son play in the back line of defense for an entire season whining the whole time about wanting to score. I put him up front and he kept going to play defense. Since it was my son I wasn't frustrated. I was mad. He admitted after a few games of trying to get him to score that he was afraid the other team would score if he didn't play back. He was probably right but that wasn't the point. He scored from midfield more than few times in the rest of the season but I never got him into a true forward position. Work with what you have and try to teach but don't downplay the good they can do.

One of the hardest habits to break may be to stop them from chasing the ball after they kick it out. When they kick it out it is the other team's throw in. The throwing team should go get the ball. That's not the way they play in the backyard or on the playground at school. Leave the ball alone unless you are going to throw it in. It will make everyone's life easier. A bad or slow exchange to the other team for their throw in could be called as delay of game or unsportsmanlike behavior. Leave it alone. Only go after it if you are the one who will throw it in.

The kickoff can seem scary to a new coach. Don't worry. The ball must travel one roll forward before another player touches it. That's it. Play two close and let one pass forward just a little to start the game. Since the other team can't be in the middle circle until after you've kicked it your player will have time to gain control and either pass or dribble as the play you set up or the situation calls for. One rotation. It must go that far. It shouldn't be sent the length of the field. That only gives the other team possession. Take advantage when you can. I see young players thrilling themselves with a long kick off but gaining nothing all the time. Work out a pass from the kickoff and you will be surprised to see the other teams doing it the next time you play. Sending from one goalie to the other may seem like good play but it's not. Play where you keep possession and it'll give your team lots of options during the game. There are a few other rules to the game that you need to know. "No handballs" speaks for itself except that the rule is from shoulder to fingertips counts as a handball. Teach that to your players early. Most don't know that an arm is off limits until they get called for it.

Off sides is tricky to learn. We'll go over it in detail in another chapter but the short version is you can't leave a player by the other team's goal to wait all game until the ball gets down there.

Depending on the age of the team you may see calls for **tripping**. You can't attack for the ball from behind. If you hit only ball in a frontal attack (tackle) the rest of what happens doesn't matter. They can collide and no call will be made. They should not try to slam an opponent but rough play is not against the rules. A takedown without touching the ball or from behind is against the rules.

You should not pass to your own goalie. Well you can but he becomes a regular player at that point and can not pick up the ball. That will not be called on a four year old but they probably won't be playing with a goalie anyway. Ask your ref if he enforces this rule before the game or the season starts. It's an actual rule but coaches of several years often scream when they get called for it the first time. Not knowing the rules is not an excuse. Some refs may not call it but others will. You will have given the other team a free shot from inside the goalie box. So ask before you start if this will be called in your league and/or age group.

Corner kicks are given to the other team when your team kicks the ball out of bounds behind the goal you are defending. The other team kicks it in from the corner. This is a good opportunity to score. Be sure to place a defender at the front goal post to keep the ball away from the front of your goal. Conversely when kicking the corner kick put a forward at the back of the goal and one in the middle in order to put the ball in the goal when it comes across. In either situation you will need to defend where the other team's players are so you need a player in all three places and more as the play unfolds. Take time to work on these. You want to take advantage when you get a corner kick and know how to limit the other team's advantage. If your team has not ever tried to do these before game time you are at a disadvantage.

Goal kicks are given when the other team kicks it out of bounds behind your goal. You kick it in from anywhere on the small box around the goal. This small box is called the six (because on a regulation field it is six yards from the goal) or goalie box. Always, always kick it toward the closest sideline. You will see the other team score from your goal kick over and over if let your goalie or defender kick it in front of the goal. Do not cross it in front of your goal until your players are strong enough to get it across the midfield line EVERYTIME. Set up that side's offensive player to come to where your goalie can kick it and settle the ball. This play will be used often. Practice it! Sooner or later your guys will start to hover where the goalie is going to kick it. If not, there needs to be more consistency with where he is kicking it. If the ball always goes to the sideline at about the same spot - your players will go there knowing they will not get the ball if they stay where they are.

Goalies, Sweepers, Strikers

Goalies are an important piece of the soccer game puzzle. I have tried everything to make mediocre goalies into outstanding players. I was coaching on the field as a ref/coach in a game that blew me away. I had put in a player I knew was a stretch for a goalie . I had worked with him as a goalie none . He didn't do anything beneficial in the field and we had kept the ball on the other side of the field almost the entire game so I moved this weak player to goal basically to get him out of the way. I walked up to him and asked him to hand me the ball. He asked" where is it?" I very calmly (not sure how I stayed calm) explained it was behind him in the net. The other team had scored on him. He turned, looked and asked "when did that happen?" He hadn't been paying attention enough to notice the ball roll right by him. Extreme? Yes. Truth? Yes. I don't know how he didn't see it. My point here is that some players just shouldn't be goalie. Don't get me wrong here. I'm all for giving everybody a chance. I'm all for trying everybody everywhere. Once you know who is not cutout for it do not make that player or the rest of the team suffer. Play them where their strengths are. Goalies in the younger league are quite often the fastest and toughest on the team. You can give basics and do goalie drills all day with a player that does not have the drive or bravery and he will be mediocre at best. The best goalies go after the ball like they are jumping on a grenade for their loved ones. I worked with a goalie all season to find out in the last game a boy who knew no basics was ten times better. He just tried harder and was braver. He would go get into the mix and come out with the ball. He played like a champion that game and we won a stunning victory that night. Look for the players that don't back down in a challenge and give them the basics. You shouldn't spend time teaching goalie techniques to a player that will not be playing that position. There is too much other stuff they should be working on.

To teach the **goalie positioning** use this illustration. Stand at midfield facing a goal. Hold your thumb up with your arm fully extended like you are telling the goal good job or you are ready. Notice how much of the goal your thumb covers up. Then bring your thumb closer to your face until it covers your eye. Notice how much of the goal your thumb covers up now? Your goalie can cover only a sliver of the goal if his heels are on the goal line. If he comes out and approaches the attacker, he can cover up the entire width of the goal. Yes the attacker may make a move and get around the goalie but ten times out of ten a player good enough to do that can make a shot into the far side of the goal where a goalie can not protect. So encourage them to go get the ball. The closer they are to the shooter the harder the shot will be. They will not be able to keep every game scoreless but the more aggressively they approach the position the more productive their time will be in the goal.

Imagine a semicircle around the face of the goal. A goalie should travel the face of the goal on this semicircle. It should come out about ten feet from the goal in the middle of the goal and end with the goalie next to a post if defending a player in the corner. The goalie that understands this positioning early will be able to protect a lot better than one who's heels are on the line. There's more room to work and the angle of the shot becomes more advantageous to the goalie than the shooter. Walk your goalie in this semi circle and get them to position themselves while you move around as a shooter in the big box. Throw balls for your goalie to catch while going from side to side for them to find the position on the semi circle.

Sweepers are great defensive weapons if you are lucky enough to have more than 6 on the field. I used a sweeper for a long time as a defensive leader. The sweeper was the one I taught about pushing up the field and offsides traps. He stays just behind the defense and helps wherever the ball comes to outman the striker. I used them as mini coaches during the game. All I had to do was remind them and they kept the other defenders in position. When your game is short sided you should not have one player in the back by himself because the other players will eventually decide it's the sweeper's job to stop the other team. Theoretically it's brilliant to use one but with only 5 fielders it is usually better to stack the middle and let your extra player be able to help offensively and defensively. Your defense will slow down the attack and allow a midfielder time to come back.

Making It Competitive

A regular Parks and Recreation team will have a wide range of skilled and not skilled players. Your job is to not only teach them to be the best they can, but also to use the players in the most beneficial ways. For example if you are playing 6v6 (six on the field at a time) with a goalie and 2 defenders then you only have a midfielder and two forwards. Having your defender perform the throw-ins frees up another forward to settle and do something with the ball. If your right forward is throwing in the ball, then no one is there for him to throw it to you will not get very far. This tip sounds obvious but the forwards want to throw-in because it is fun and they expect someone else to do their job when they do. I see it every game. It can mean the difference between a score and a possession change.

Try the players in **different positions**. For some reason being close to the goal gets some players' hearts racing. Some will play harder as a forward/striker. Some play harder to prevent a goal. Swap them up early to find a working strategy and then stick with it. If you move them too much during the season the momentum will be lost and you'll regret it.

Be the moron coach that **encourages too much**! I believe this has as much to do with changing the way your team plays as giving them instruction. I have seen teams that had no real talent make it farther than they ever would have hoped in the year-end tournaments. I coached a team of low skilled players that made it all the way to the District Tournament on their drive alone. None of the players magically turned into a MLS bound superstar but they all worked so hard they made things happen for themselves. I can't emphasize this enough. If you feel like you are going overboard with encouragement – you might be doing it enough. A lot of the players will get in the car after the game to a parent telling them every little thing they did wrong. Most of the time they won't even remember the play their parent is criticizing. Too much happens in an hour long game to remember every kick, fast break, or missed opportunity. Yelling good things from the sideline will make them want to do their best for YOU! It will motivate the players that are hesitant to get in there and fight for the ball. It will be a good platform for you to say "hey that was awesome – next time turn your body so the player stays on the sideline instead of breaking in the middle toward the goal." Even if you tell them after the game about that scenario they won't remember that play, but if you have them listening for encouragement after plays they will be receptive for coaching.

Give your team the goals you want them to achieve. Don't just sit quietly back and hope they get better at this or that. Set up the drills that enforce it and tell them that this is what we are working on because we need to do better in this situation. Depending on the age and maturity of your players this can really help. **Setting expectations** for something will make your team focus on it during the game or the practice. I set expectations for more passing one game in particular and the players pulled off an upset of monumental proportions! (It was 10 year olds – so imagine the celebration afterwards.) I asked them to pass at least once before every shot. I knew we were facing a goalie that was exceptional. He was leading the league because he attacked every ball in the box. By setting the expectations to pass before the shot I changed the way they saw the problem. I told them not to shoot unless they were passed the ball by one of our players and that set up a lot of opportunities. The goalie was in their face as soon as they dribbled into the box. The goal was left wide open every time from the other side of the box. It made the other guys go play support since they knew the one who dribbled up could not shoot. It totally changed the way the other coach had to play the game.

He moved his better players back to defense instead of being forwards. Since we were ahead when he did that there was not much chance of him scoring. Tell your kids what you are trying to accomplish. If you have been encouraging they will try to do it.

Emphasize the win but **don't focus on the loss**. Other parents have come to me with with complaints about their coach in this area. If you degrade your team after a loss they will quite often freeze up in tough situations. They are young and feel the criticism to their bones if not done right. Tell them the things they did right and a few things to work on. Don't dwell on the mishaps. Keeping the tone light after a loss shows them that you care about them not just the score. Do not avoid the criticism but do not single out a player. Use it as a way to work on those aspects rather than a rant on you were not trying hard enough.

Discipline and Parent Engagement

Very few things can keep the attention of a little monster like a fast pace. You can't always keep the pace at lightning speed but the more time allow for nonsense the more there will be. Even kids that do not normally join in the nonsense will be tempted if left to their own devices for too long. In practices keep the huddled discussions short. Making sure everyone is on one knee and paying attention before you start talking will pay off big time. When you see them getting restless put them to work. You may only have an hour with them to practice so use it on the drills, games, and other fun stuff in the next chapter. Age will determine if you have them run laps for things like handballs in practice. It might not be a good idea for a 6 year old to do laps, but a ten year old will learn the lesson if they are running a lap while the rest of the team is playing a "game/drill". I try to warn a few times and then if they still have the habit of reaching for the ball then make the laps a lesson.

Expectations are important. I try to set expectations from the start. If a player or group of players get in my face asking to play a certain position I'll make a note of what they want but tell them if you act that way I can't put you there. Make sure you do not reward that behavior. Let them try that position later that game or the next. If it was fairly certain they would be in that position they wouldn't be acting that way to begin with. Discourage the behaviors that are over the top and tell them "our team" does not act that way. I've had a few that I thought I might not be able to handle but I kept them busy. They either did what I told them or they went to sit with their parents. I had one that really should not have been there. He wouldn't leave his dad's side for the world. He sat down on his dad's foot when I asked him to join the team. I discussed the problem with his parents during one practice. I explained he would not get to play like the kids that worked if he would not work. His parents wanted him to play but he did not want to. He was not quite mature enough for that team. The rules were that every child got to play 1/2 the game. Those were some rough games. Luckily he didn't show up much since he did not want to be there. He stayed in trouble and the parents wouldn't help me. I made it through it by not rewarding him except when he did what I wanted. I made sure to put him in the positions he didn't like until he started acting like a person rather than a monster. Eventually he did act like a person. It took a while. He never became a decent player but when he started trying the behavior changed. He wanted some of the recognition I was giving the other players. He actually earned some by his behavior but not even a little from his play.

Setting up a discussion with the parents before the first practice can help set expectations. Making sure they know that you expect to have fun and learn this season sets their mind to ease. Tell them how you do not expect too much but do expect them to try. Also explain that you are a volunteer and would appreciate any help they would be able to give. Ask for a "team mom or dad" to set up the snack schedule and get it to everyone. You will put in a lot of time so if you can delegate a little work – do it!

Rules

Its better you chose soccer to coach than most sports. The rules are simple. I'll go through the main ones here and if your area plays with any other rules that aren't the universal ones you can discuss them with your Park and Rec leader. Age will play into this as well but most rules are pretty clear.

No Hands! Ok this one is self-explanatory except that is considered a handball from your shoulder to your fingertips. Since this one is so easy I'll take it another step here and explain advantage calls. If, for example, your team commits a hand ball when it would hurt the other team to stop the play and give them a free kick the ref will not make the call. It's a lot like declining the penalty in football. The ref makes an on the fly decision. They don't always get this right. This might be why you see penalties not being called. You wouldn't want them calling the other team for a handball if it stops your fast break! Don't be rough on a ref if you see a missed call. Sometimes they didn't make the call in order to help you keep an advantage. The younger teams will get the younger refs. They do this so the more experienced refs can call the more intense older kid games. It gives the younger refs experience. If you run off all the young refs you won't have good refs for your games in a few years. Think about it. Running off inexperienced one just makes a hole for more even less experienced to fill.

No Tripping! Here it gets a little confusing but the simple take away is nothing with your hands, arms, or from behind. If you see an overly aggressive player knocking down your players you have to look further. Players will fall down. As long as the contest is from the front and they connect with the ball it is legal. They cannot use their hands or arms to push or pull a player. I see rough play all the time. Parents get upset. Coaches get upset. Before you go off the handle remember this is a rougher sport than many realize. If it's done in the right way you can slide feet first into the ball and it be legal. It looks like a tripping call should be whistled but if the ball is contacted first you don't have a leg to stand on. The pun was intended. It is completely legal to slide into the ball and an opposing player as long as you hit the ball first. This must not be done from behind however. It may even call for a yellow or red card if done from behind. One yellow is a warning. The next yellow is equivalent to a red card and that player will be expelled from that game. He will also be forced to sit out the next game. Make sure you stop this behavior in practice so it doesn't go into a game.

Don't be **offsides!** This one is harder to understand. Offsides is when your player has gotten behind the last defensive player AND is involved with the play. For instance if your player is even one step closer to the other goal than the last defender (not including the goalie) then receives a pass he is considered offsides. It stops you from leaving a player beside the goal and making them defend the whole field. Teach your players to not let themselves be closer to the goal they are attacking than the last defender. That's not to say they can't dribble past the defender. They just can't be past them when the ball is kicked to them. Check out diagram for a visual. The last defender (not including the goalie) would be the offsides line (X) and offensive player couldn't pass to oblong circle because he is past that line. Circle could dribble all the way into the goal but if he includes the one across the offsides line in the play a penalty will be called.

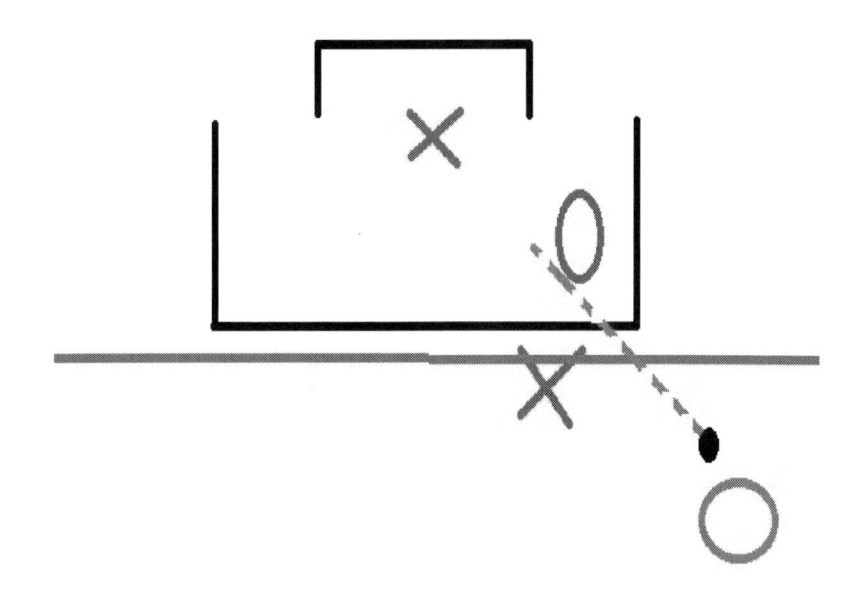

The goalies area of operation includes the two boxes around the goal. The smallest is called the goal box or the six yard line. The largest is the penalty box or the 18 (because on a regulation field it is 18 yards from the goal). Remember goal kicks are taken from anywhere on the goalie box. The goalie can pick up the ball anywhere inside penalty box. They can not cross the penalty box line while holding the ball. When they leave the penalty box they are considered a regular player. Another rule you may be called on is if your player passes to your goalie then he can't pick it up. He is considered a regular player for that play. He must use only his feet to clear it away.

Kick offs must travel forward one full revolution before touched by another player. The kicker can not touch the ball again until another player has touched it. He can not kick off to himself.

Free kick vs Penalty Kick -

A free kick is given for such rule infractions as tripping, handball, and offsides. The ball is placed stationary in the spot of the foul. The referee will signal with an arm pointing down when it is a "direct kick" and up when it is an "indirect kick". If indirect the ball will need to touch two players before going into the goal. When an infraction happens against the defensive team inside the penalty box it is placed on the dot in front of the goal. The main thing to remember here is the goalie will be the only person other than the kicker allowed in the box until after the ball is kicked. Yes. It's a one on one. Don't handball in your own penalty box!

Games, Drills, Fun and Useful

I mentioned a few games earlier in the book like Sharks and Minnows. These games can get the players moving with a ball at their feet and they love doing it. It's a win – win. A good opening drill for practice is the Hat Dance. With a ball in front of you touch the top of the ball with your right then left foot. See how many times they can do it in 30 seconds. See who won. Do it again. This works on coordination and endurance. Follow with Bellringer. With the ball between your feet swing your feet back and forth a bell ringing without going forward. Keep score. Do it again. These will also give your monsters something to do at home by themselves. After doing those for a few minutes have your players practice juggling the ball on their knee. They will not be able to until they are close to 6 or 7. Using knee, foot, and head they should be able to keep it in the air for 5 or more juggles. This will help with coordination in a big way when they are trying to settle a pass in the game.

I love to play this little game with the younger ones because they really enjoy it and are learning so fast. I call it Jargon Run. I pick a marking on the field and ask the kids to race to it. I have them all line up on the midfield line. I yell Goalie box and they all race to be the first to sit on the goalie box line. Once they are all there I yell End line (see diagram for the parts of the field so you can do this drill to.) I'll pick another term or two and then repeat them. Once they know all the spots on the field – the 18 or the 6. I'll move on to other drills but when trying to tell them where to go it helps if you and they know the marks on the field. You can do this drill with or without a ball but as long as it is a race they will they will try to remember the parts of the field and get moving. Using a ball to get more dribbling practice is good once they have done this drill a few times.

Another fast and fun drill is a lot like musical chairs but instead of running around chairs they have to get and keep possession of a ball. I start them lined up on the midfield line and put one less ball than there are players inside the six (goalie box). Have them take off on your "go". The one without a ball when you count down to zero is out. I usually give them 10 seconds to run down the field and fight over the ball. If a ball goes out of the six it doesn't count any more. Only players with a ball and inside the six get to move to the next round. Take away the same number of balls as players eliminated and go until there is only one left. The players will run like the monster from "IT" is chasing them in this one. It will help them on conditioning, ball control, attacking for the ball, and protecting the ball.

I try to use the cone maze with gates I talked about earlier at least once per practice. When I've finished with that drill I change the cones to make 4 boxes about 10 yards apart. (see diagram)

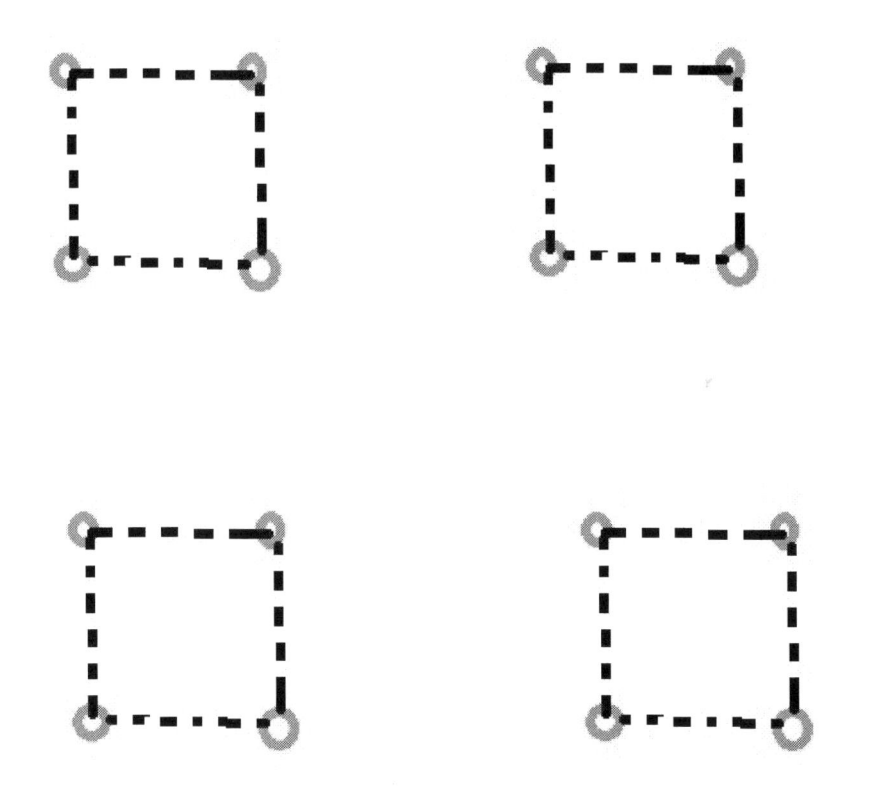

I learned this one in a coaching seminar about 10 years ago. They put us through the paces and I thought I was I going to die. I was in shape running half marathons back then, but I couldn't keep up with the pace of this game. The kids grow so much with this one. See the diagram and it will make sense but instead of shooting at a goal, in this game they pass the ball into one of the boxes and their partner stops the ball with control. If they complete a pass that is "settled" by their teammate they get a point. I usually throw the ball in the middle and let them fight over it to start each round. 4 players at a time are in the field and it only takes a few seconds to get to 2 or 3 points. They will be ready for a water break soon because this drill is exhaustive.

Epilogue

There is no reason for anyone to shy away from coaching soccer. The game is simple and fun. The kids will be eternally grateful for the time and energy you spend. I hope this book has given you the confidence to run out on the field and get started. The main things to remember are: Keep the players moving for the whole practice, make it competitive, be encouraging, have fun! If you will keep those things in mind while on the field it will go smoothly. A little practice for the players and the coach will show through in big ways!

Made in the USA
Columbia, SC
22 September 2021